T0199018

Lanie Loves Books

Becki Bickett

Illustrated by Shannen Marie Paradero

WestBow Press books may be ordered through booksellers or by contacting:

WestBow Press
A Division of Thomas Nelson & Zondervan
1663 Liberty Drive
Bloomington, IN 47403
www.westbowpress.com
844.714.3454

ISBN: 978-1-6642-0230-6 (sc)
ISBN: 978-1-6642-0232-0 (hc)
ISBN: 978-1-6642-0231-3 (e)

Library of Congress Control Number: 2020915467

Print information available on the last page.

WestBow Press rev. date: 10/27/2020

WESTBOW
PRESS®
A DIVISION OF THOMAS NELSON
& ZONDERVAN

Preface - background on Lanie Loves Series

This book is dedicated to my son and his wife, Josh and Mary, who waited with great expectation to receive their firstborn child, Lanie Grace, into their home September 2013. However, our hearts were broken when Lanie's little heart unexpectedly stopped on May 30th.

This book is in honor of our little Lanie, and for all families who have suffered such great loss. May you find joy in the imagination of what may have been and what may be again one day.

To all readers: Lanie was known as our little "Laniebug" before she was taken and ladybugs represent her memory to this day. In addition to the story, be sure to spend a little extra time in that reading cuddle and search out the little ladybug hidden on every page.

Hi! I'm Lanie and I'm 3 years old!

And I LOVE to read books!

I love to read books every day
and in so many places!

Like in my secret fort.
Shhhh...it is our secret.

When I go outside I love to bring my books with me.

Sometimes we have a picnic and I read my books to all my friends.

I sometimes play in my treehouse
and I read there too!

When I ride my bike, my books always go with me.

Now it is time to go inside and get ready for my bath.

Time for bed!

But when I wake up in the morning - guess what I am going to do?

That's right!! I'm going to read my books!

Did you have fun finding all the ladybugs?

Let's count them again.

1   2   3   4   5   6   7   8   9   10

Printed in the United States
By Bookmasters